Better Homes and Gardens®

FISH & SEAFOOD

Our seal assures you that every recipe in *Fish and Seafood*
has been tested in the Better Homes and Gardens® Test Kitchen.
This means that each recipe is practical and reliable, and
meets our high standards of taste appeal.

For years, Better Homes and Gardens® Books has been a leader in publishing cook books. In *Fish and Seafood,* we've pulled together a delicious collection of recipes from several of our latest best-sellers. These no-fail recipes will make your cooking easier and more enjoyable.

Editor: Rosemary C. Hutchinson
Editorial Project Manager: Rosanne Weber Mattson
Graphic Designer: Harijs Priekulis
Electronic Text Processor: Paula Forest

On the front cover: Wine-Poached Fish with Vegetable Sauce (see recipe, 18)

Contents

Pizza-Baked Rockfish

Pizza-Baked Rockfish

8 ounces fresh *or* frozen
  skinless rockfish *or*
  red snapper fillets
½ cup sliced fresh mushrooms
¼ cup chopped onion
¼ cup water
3 tablespoons tomato paste
½ teaspoon dried basil,
  crushed
½ teaspoon dried oregano,
  crushed
¼ teaspoon sugar
¼ teaspoon fennel seed
⅛ teaspoon crushed red
  pepper
1 clove garlic, minced
  Nonstick spray coating
4 green pepper rings
½ cup shredded mozzarella
  cheese (2 ounces)

● Thaw fish, if frozen. For sauce, in a small saucepan combine *half* of the mushrooms, onion, water, tomato paste, basil, oregano, sugar, fennel seed, red pepper, and garlic. Bring to boiling, then reduce heat. Simmer, uncovered, for 4 minutes, stirring the mixture occasionally. Remove from heat.

● Meanwhile, spray 2 shallow individual casseroles with the nonstick coating. Measure thickness of fish. Cut it into 2 equal portions. Place fish in casseroles, tucking under any thin edges.

● Spoon the sauce over fish. Top with remaining mushrooms, green pepper, and cheese. Bake in a 450° oven till fish is done (allow 5 to 7 minutes per ½-inch thickness). Makes 2 servings.

Snowcapped Grouper

Serve steamed broccoli as a colorful companion to this puffy egg-topped fish.

1 pound fresh *or* frozen
  skinless grouper, salmon,
  sea bass, *or* tile-fish
  fillets (½ to ¾ inch thick)
  Nonstick spray coating
1 tablespoon all-purpose flour
2 egg whites
¼ cup mayonnaise *or* salad
  dressing
½ teaspoon dry mustard
3 tablespoons grated
  Parmesan cheese

● Thaw fish, if frozen. Spray a 12x7½x2-inch baking dish with nonstick coating. Cut fish into 4 equal portions. Dip fish into flour, then place in baking dish; tuck under any thin edges.

● For egg topping, beat egg whites till stiff peaks form (tips stand straight). Combine mayonnaise or salad dressing and mustard, then fold it into egg whites. Spoon egg topping on fish. Sprinkle with cheese. Bake in a 350° oven for 25 to 30 minutes or till topping is golden and fish is done. Makes 4 servings.

To micro-cook: Prepare Snowcapped Grouper as above, *except* do not dip fish in flour. Place fish in dish. Cover with vented plastic wrap. Micro-cook on 100% power (high) for 3 minutes. Rotate dish a half-turn. Cook on high for 2 to 4 minutes or till done; drain. Spoon on egg topping. Sprinkle with cheese. Cook, uncovered, on 50% power (medium) for 8 to 10 minutes or till egg is soft-set, rotating dish a quarter-turn every 3 minutes.

Sole en Papillote

Paper cookery at its best—elegant, easy, and low-fat.

1 to 1¼ pounds fresh *or* frozen sole *or* other fish fillets
¼ cup dry vermouth
  Nonstick spray coating
2 cups sliced fresh mushrooms
2 green onions, sliced
4 15x12-inch pieces parchment paper
1 tablespoon margarine, melted
  Pepper
4 lemon slices

● Thaw fish, if frozen. Cut into four pieces. Place fish in a shallow dish, then add vermouth. Cover and marinate in the refrigerator for 1 hour. Spray a skillet with nonstick coating. Cook mushrooms and onions in the skillet till tender.

● Remove fish from vermouth. Add vermouth to mushroom mixture. Cook mixture over medium heat till liquid evaporates. Meanwhile, fold each piece of parchment paper in half lengthwise, then cut a half-heart shape on the folded edge.

● To assemble, open one parchment heart and brush *half* of it with some melted margarine. Place one fish portion on the brushed half of heart, cutting fillet as necessary to fit. Top with ¼ of the mushroom mixture, then sprinkle with pepper. Place lemon slice on the fillet. Fold paper and seal the package, as shown on the opposite page, making four bundles total. Place bundles on a baking sheet.

● Bake in a 450° oven about 10 minutes or until paper puffs up. *Or,* carefully unwrap paper and test with a fork for doneness. Slit bundles; transfer to serving plates. Makes 4 servings.

Nonstick Spray Coating

A slick way to save fat, cholesterol, and calories during cooking is to use nonstick spray coating.

Several brands of nonstick spray coating are now available, and each product description is a little different. On your grocer's shelf you may find this nonstick cooking product marked as "natural vegetable coating," "vegetable or corn oil cooking spray," or simply "cooking spray."

Regardless of the description, all of the sprays contain vegetable oil. Read the label to discover additional ingredients.

Basically, the fat-saving concept is to eliminate the need for cooking oil. When you spray a small amount of nonstick coating onto a skillet or baking dish, it forms a very thin film that prevents food from sticking.

Be sure to read and follow the directions before using any of these products.

1 Folding the Sole en Papillote

After arranging the fish, mushroom mixture, and lemon slice on half of a section of parchment paper, seal the package by carefully folding the edges together in a double fold. Fold only a small section of the parchment paper at a time to ensure a tight seal. This allows the fish to steam in the enclosed package.

You also can use brown paper as a suitable alternative to parchment paper. Look for both kinds of paper at kitchen shops or in the paper section of your grocery store.

2 Serving the fish bundles

During baking, the parchment paper will puff up and become light brown. This is a good sign that the fish is done.

Just before serving, slit open the top of each packet with a small scissors or sharp knife and let the steam escape. Place each packet on a serving plate. That way diners can enjoy the fun of opening their own packets by tearing gently at the slits.

Easy Halibut Wellington

4 fresh *or* frozen halibut, shark, *or* swordfish steaks, cut 1 inch thick (1¼ pounds)
1 cup finely chopped fresh mushrooms
1 green onion, sliced
1 tablespoon butter *or* margarine
1 beaten egg yolk
¼ teaspoon dried dillweed
Dash salt
Dash pepper
1 package (8) refrigerated crescent rolls
1 slightly beaten egg white

● Thaw fish, if frozen. For filling, in saucepan cook mushrooms and green onion in butter for 4 to 5 minutes or till vegetables are tender, stirring constantly. Remove from heat and cool slightly. Stir in egg yolk, dillweed, salt, and pepper.

● Remove skin and bones from fish. In a medium skillet bring ½ cup *water* just to boiling. Carefully add fish. Return just to boiling, then reduce the heat. Cover and simmer gently for 6 minutes (fish will *not* be done). Remove fish from water. Pat fish dry with paper towels.

● Unroll crescent rolls. Seal perforations to form 4 rectangles. On a lightly floured surface roll each into a rectangle about 2 inches longer and 2 inches wider than the steaks.

● To assemble, place fish in a greased shallow baking pan. Spoon the mushroom filling on top. Then top with the pastry rectangles, tucking the pastry edges under about ½ inch. (To prevent sogginess, do not wrap entire steak in pastry.) Brush with egg white. Bake in a 425° oven about 10 minutes or till pastry is golden brown and fish is done. Makes 4 servings.

Salmon en Croûte

2 ¾-pound fresh *or* frozen skinless salmon fillets (¾ to 1 inch thick)
1 10-ounce package frozen chopped spinach
2 green onions, sliced
1 tablespoon butter *or* margarine
¼ cup fine dry seasoned bread crumbs
1 beaten egg yolk
½ of a 17½-ounce package (1 sheet) frozen puff pastry, thawed
1 beaten egg
1 tablespoon water
1 package Hollandaise sauce mix

● Thaw fish, if frozen. For filling, cook spinach according to package directions. Drain well, pressing out excess liquid. In a skillet cook the green onions in butter till tender but not brown. Stir in bread crumbs and egg yolk, then stir in spinach.

● In a large skillet bring 2 cups *water* just to boiling. Carefully add fish. Return just to boiling, then reduce heat. Cover and simmer gently for 2 minutes (fish will *not* be done). Remove fish from water. Pat fish dry with paper towels.

● On a floured surface roll pastry into a rectangle about 4 inches longer than length of a fillet. Lay fillets side by side; measure width. Roll pastry to twice the width *plus* 2 inches.

● Transfer pastry to an ungreased 15x10x1-inch baking pan. On *half* of the rectangle, spread *half* of the filling to within 1 inch of edges. Top with fish, then with remaining filling. Combine egg and water; brush onto pastry edges. Bring pastry over fish. Seal edges with a fork. Brush top with remaining egg mixture. Bake in a 400° oven for 20 to 25 minutes or till golden. Meanwhile, prepare Hollandaise sauce mix according to package directions. Serve fish with sauce. Makes 6 servings.

Impress dinner guests with Salmon en Croûte—salmon and spinach enclosed in a flaky crust.

1 Assembling the salmon bundle

Transfer the rolled-out pastry to an ungreased 15x10x1-inch baking pan, laying it across an edge as shown at right. Spread *half* of the filling over *half* of the rectangle to within 1 inch of the edges. Place the fillets on top of the filling, fitting the fillets together to form a rectangle. Then spread the remaining filling evenly over both fillets.

2 Sealing the pastry

Brush the egg-water mixture onto the edges of the pastry. (The mixture helps keep the pastry firmly sealed.) Then bring the pastry over to cover the fish. If necessary, trim the edges so they meet evenly. Seal by pressing edges together with the tines of a fork.

Basil-Buttered Steaks
(grilled version)

Sesame-Dill Shark

Toasted sesame seed not only adds a nutty flavor, but garnishes the steaks, too.

3 fresh *or* frozen shark, halibut, salmon, *or* swordfish steaks, cut 1 inch thick (about 1½ pounds)
2 teaspoons finely shredded lemon peel
¼ cup lemon juice
2 tablespoons cooking oil
1 teaspoon dried dillweed
2 teaspoons sesame seed, toasted

● Thaw fish, if frozen. Place fish in a baking dish large enough to hold the fish in a single layer. For the marinade, combine lemon peel, lemon juice, cooking oil, and dillweed. Pour over fish. Turn fish to coat it with marinade. Cover; marinate fish in the refrigerator for 4 to 6 hours, turning fish over occasionally.

● Drain the fish, reserving the marinade. Place fish on a greased rack of an unheated broiler pan. Brush with some reserved marinade. Broil 4 inches from the heat for 5 minutes. Using a wide spatula, carefully turn the fish over. Brush with more marinade. Broil for 3 to 7 minutes more or till fish is done.

● To serve, brush with marinade and sprinkle with toasted sesame seed. Makes 3 servings.

To grill: Prepare Sesame-Dill Shark as directed above, *except* brush grill rack with *cooking oil.* Place fish on rack. Brush fish with marinade. Grill fish on an uncovered grill directly over *medium-hot* coals for 5 minutes. Carefully turn fish over. Brush with more marinade and grill for 3 to 7 minutes more or till fish is done. Brush with marinade and sprinkle with sesame seed.

Basil-Buttered Steaks

"The simpler, the better" describes these grilled steaks topped with an herb butter.

4 fresh *or* frozen halibut, salmon, shark, *or* swordfish steaks, cut 1 inch thick (about 2 pounds)
½ cup butter *or* margarine, softened
1 tablespoon snipped fresh basil *or* 1 teaspoon dried basil, crushed
1 tablespoon snipped parsley
2 teaspoons lemon juice

● Thaw fish, if frozen. For butter mixture, in a small bowl mix butter, basil, parsley, and lemon juice till well blended.

● Place the fish on a greased rack of an unheated broiler pan. Lightly brush fish with some of the butter mixture. Broil 4 inches from the heat for 5 minutes. Then, using a wide spatula, carefully turn fish over. Lightly brush with more of the butter mixture. Broil for 3 to 7 minutes more or till fish is done.

● To serve, dollop remaining butter mixture on top of fish. Makes 4 servings.

To grill: Prepare Basil-Buttered Steaks as directed above, *except* brush grill rack with *cooking oil.* Place fish on rack. Lightly brush fish with butter mixture. Grill fish on an uncovered grill directly over *medium-hot* coals for 5 minutes. Carefully turn fish over. Lightly brush with more butter mixture and grill for 3 to 7 minutes more or till fish is done. Dollop remaining butter mixture on top of fish.

Citrus-Marinated Fillets

When buying blocks of frozen fish, make sure they're solidly frozen and that the package sides are straight, not curved in or out. The package should be tightly sealed and show no signs of frost.

1 **pound fresh *or* frozen fish fillets**
⅓ **cup water**
⅓ **cup lime juice**
2 **tablespoons honey**
1 **tablespoon cooking oil**
½ **teaspoon dried dillweed**
¼ **teaspoon salt**

● Thaw fish, if frozen. Separate fillets or cut into 4 serving-size portions. Place fish in a shallow pan.

● For marinade, combine the water, lime juice, honey, cooking oil, dried dillweed, and salt. Pour marinade over fish portions. Cover and refrigerate for 3 to 24 hours; turn fish occasionally.

● Remove the fish from the pan, reserving marinade. Place the fish on the greased rack of an unheated broiler pan, tucking under any thin edges so the fish will be uniform in thickness and cook evenly.

● Broil fish 4 inches from heat till fish flakes easily when tested with a fork (see photograph, below). (Allow 5 minutes for each ½ inch of thickness; if fish pieces are more than 1 inch thick, turn halfway through cooking time.) Baste fish often with reserved marinade during broiling. Brush fish with marinade just before serving. Makes 4 servings.

Testing fish for doneness
To check fish for doneness, insert fork tines into the fish at a 45-degree angle. Twist the fork gently. At the just-done stage, the fish will flake apart easily, as shown, and the flesh will be opaque white.

If fish resists flaking and still has a translucent, pinkish white color, it is not done. A dry and mealy texture indicates that the fish is overcooked.

Herb-Marinated Grouper

Good 'n' herby with just a hint of hotness.

10 ounces fresh *or* frozen
    skinless grouper fillets
    or steaks
½ cup dry white wine
 2 tablespoons olive oil *or*
    cooking oil
 1 green onion, sliced
 1 small clove garlic, minced
½ teaspoon dried basil,
    crushed
¼ teaspoon salt
¼ teaspoon dried oregano,
    crushed
⅛ teaspoon crushed red
    pepper

● Thaw fish, if frozen. Measure thickness of fish. Place fish in a baking dish large enough to hold the fish in a single layer.

● For marinade, combine wine, oil, onion, garlic, basil, salt, oregano, and red pepper. Pour over fish. Turn fish to coat it with marinade. Cover and marinate fish in the refrigerator for 4 to 6 hours, turning fish over occasionally.

● Drain fish, reserving marinade. Place fish on a greased rack of an unheated broiler pan. Brush fish with some of the reserved marinade. Broil 4 inches from the heat till the fish is done, brushing occasionally with the marinade. (Allow 4 to 6 minutes per ½-inch thickness of fish.) If fish is 1 inch or more thick, carefully turn it over halfway through broiling. Serves 2.

To grill: Prepare Herb-Marinated Grouper as above, *except* place fish in a well-greased wire grill basket. Brush with marinade, then close basket. Grill on an uncovered grill directly over *medium-hot* coals till done, brushing occasionally with marinade. (Allow 4 to 6 minutes per ½-inch thickness of fish.) If fish is 1 inch or more thick, turn it over halfway through grilling.

Teriyaki Halibut

When you're grilling a flaky fish like halibut, use a wire grill basket for easy turning.

 2 fresh *or* frozen halibut,
    shark, *or* tuna steaks,
    cut 1 inch thick (about
    1 pound)
¼ cup soy sauce
 2 tablespoons sake *or* dry
    sherry
 1 tablespoon sugar
 1 teaspoon dry mustard
 1 teaspoon grated gingerroot
 2 cloves garlic, minced

● Thaw fish, if frozen. Place fish in a baking dish large enough to hold the fish in a single layer. For the marinade, combine soy sauce, sake or dry sherry, sugar, mustard, gingerroot, and garlic. Pour over fish. Turn fish to coat. Cover; marinate fish in the refrigerator for 4 to 6 hours, turning fish over occasionally.

● Drain fish, reserving marinade. Place fish on a greased rack of an unheated broiler pan. Brush fish with some of the reserved marinade. Broil 4 inches from the heat for 5 minutes. Using a wide spatula, carefully turn fish over. Brush with more of the marinade and broil for 3 to 7 minutes more or till fish is done. Brush with marinade before serving. Makes 2 servings.

To grill: Prepare Teriyaki Halibut as directed above, *except* brush grill rack with *cooking oil*. Place fish on rack. Brush fish with marinade. Grill fish on an uncovered grill directly over *medium-hot* coals for 5 minutes. Carefully turn fish over. Brush with more marinade and grill for 3 to 7 minutes more or till fish is done. Brush with marinade before serving.

Gingered Plum-Glazed Halibut

Just one bite and you're off to the Orient! The sweet 'n' sour glaze, with its touch of hotness, is what sends you on your way.

4 fresh *or* frozen halibut, shark, *or* swordfish steaks, cut 1 inch thick (about 2 pounds)
¾ cup red plum jam
1 tablespoon vinegar
½ teaspoon grated gingerroot *or* ⅛ teaspoon ground ginger
½ teaspoon crushed red pepper
⅛ teaspoon garlic powder
Cooking oil

● Thaw fish, if frozen. For glaze, in a small saucepan combine plum jam, vinegar, gingerroot, red pepper, and garlic powder. Bring to boiling, stirring constantly. Remove from heat.

● Place the fish on a greased rack of an unheated broiler pan. Lightly brush fish with cooking oil. Broil 4 inches from the heat for 5 minutes. Using a wide spatula, carefully turn fish over. Lightly brush fish with more cooking oil. Broil for 3 to 7 minutes more or till done, brushing fish with some of the glaze the last 2 minutes of broiling. Pass the remaining glaze. Serves 4.

To grill: Prepare the Gingered-Plum-Glazed Halibut as directed above, *except* brush grill rack with cooking oil. Place fish on rack. Lightly brush fish with cooking oil. Grill on an uncovered grill directly over *medium-hot* coals for 5 minutes. Carefully turn fish over and lightly brush with more cooking oil. Grill for 3 to 7 minutes more or till done, brushing fish with some of the glaze the last 2 minutes. Pass remaining glaze.

Orange-Cumin Tuna

Orange twists and parsley dress up these glistening steaks.

4 fresh *or* frozen tuna *or* swordfish steaks, cut ½ inch thick (about 1 pound)
2 teaspoons cornstarch
1 teaspoon brown sugar
⅛ teaspoon ground cumin
Dash salt
¾ cup orange juice
Nonstick spray coating
1 tablespoon olive oil *or* cooking oil
Orange slices (optional)
Parsley sprigs (optional)

● Thaw fish, if frozen. For sauce, in a small saucepan combine cornstarch, sugar, cumin, and salt. Stir in orange juice. Cook and stir till thickened and bubbly. Cook and stir for 2 minutes more. Remove from heat. Cover to keep warm while fish cooks.

● Spray the *cold* rack of an unheated broiler pan with nonstick coating. Place fish on the rack. Brush fish with the oil. Broil 4 inches from the heat for 4 to 6 minutes or till fish is done.

● To serve, transfer fish to a platter. Spoon sauce over fish. If desired, garnish with orange twists and parsley. Serves 4.

To grill: Prepare Orange-Cumin Tuna as directed above, *except* spray the *cold* grill rack with nonstick coating. Place fish on rack. Brush fish with the oil. Grill on an uncovered grill directly over *medium-hot* coals for 4 to 6 minutes or till fish is done. Serve as above.

Five-Spice Smoked Fish

Turn your full-size grill into a smoker.

1 3- to 4-pound fresh *or* frozen
    dressed cod, pollack,
    red snapper, *or* sea trout
2 cups applewood *or* Osage
    orangewood chips, *or* 4 to
    6 mesquite chunks
1 teaspoon ground cinnamon
1 teaspoon aniseed, crushed,
    or 1 star anise, crushed
½ teaspoon salt
¼ teaspoon fennel seed,
    crushed
¼ teaspoon coarse ground
    pepper *or* Szechuan
    pepper
⅛ teaspoon ground cloves
1 tablespoon cooking oil

● Thaw fish, if frozen. 1 hour before cooking, soak the wood in enough *water* to cover. Meanwhile, using a sharp knife, cut ½-inch-deep diagonal slits, 1 inch apart, into both sides of fish.

● For the seasoning mixture, combine cinnamon, aniseed, salt, fennel seed, pepper, and cloves. Rub fish cavity with some of the seasoning mixture. Rub oil into slits. Then rub the remaining seasonings on outside of fish, pressing seasonings into the slits.

● Tear off a piece of *heavy* foil large enough to hold fish. Prick a few holes in the foil. Drain the wood. To smoke-cook the fish, in a covered grill arrange preheated coals around a foil drip pan. (The fish is too large to fit in a water smoker.) Test for *medium* heat above the pan. Place the drained wood on the preheated coals. Place fish on foil on the rack over center of drip pan, but not over coals. Lower grill hood. Grill for 40 to 50 minutes or till fish is done. Makes 6 to 8 servings.

Preparing the fish
Use a dressed fish or remove the head and tail from a drawn fish. Otherwise, the fish will be too large to fit on the grill rack.

    Cut ½-inch-deep diagonal slits about 1 inch apart on both sides of the fish. During smoke-cooking, the fish will absorb the blend of the spices through these slits.

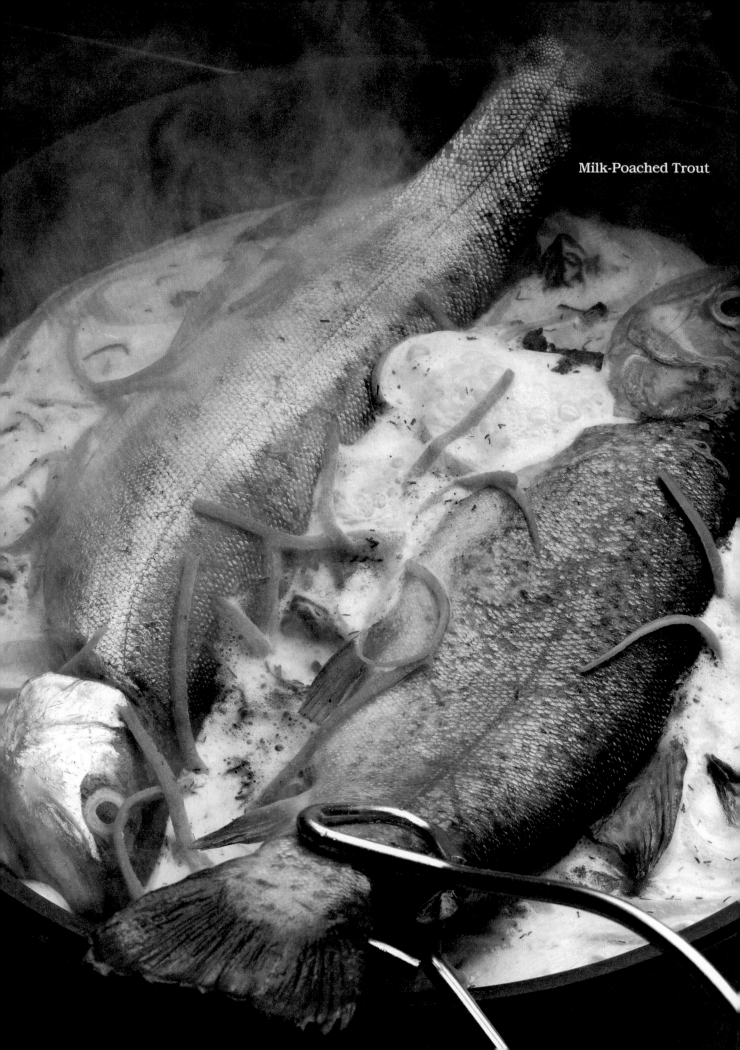

Milk-Poached Trout

Sole Véronique

Pronounce it vay-raw-NEEK. This classic French dish is named after the Veronica seedless grape, but any seedless grape will do.

1 pound fresh *or* frozen
    skinless sole, Atlantic
    ocean perch, cusk,
    flounder, *or* whitefish
    fillets
1 cup chicken broth
⅓ cup milk
1 tablespoon all-purpose flour
½ teaspoon finely shredded
    lemon peel
    Dash ground nutmeg
½ cup seedless grapes, halved
    Watercress sprigs (optional)

● Thaw fish, if frozen. Measure thickness of fish. In a large skillet bring the chicken broth just to boiling. Carefully add fish. Return just to boiling, then reduce heat. Cover and simmer gently till done (allow 4 to 6 minutes per ½-inch thickness of fish). Transfer fish to a serving platter. Cover fish to keep it warm while preparing sauce.

● For sauce, gently boil broth, uncovered, till reduced to ½ *cup*. Combine milk, flour, lemon peel, and nutmeg. Then add to broth. Cook and stir over medium heat till thickened and bubbly. Add grapes. Cook and stir for 1 minute more. Pour sauce over fish. If desired, garnish with watercress. Serves 4.

Milk-Poached Trout

Use lots of vegetables and herbs to season this poaching liquid. Then add hints of sherry and paprika to enhance the flavor and color of the sauce.

2 8- to 10-ounce fresh *or*
    frozen scaled drawn
    rainbow trout *or* coho
    salmon
¾ cup milk
½ cup water
1 small onion, sliced and
    separated into rings
1 small carrot, cut into
    julienne sticks
¼ cup celery leaves
¾ teaspoon dried dillweed
½ teaspoon salt
⅛ teaspoon pepper
1 tablespoon cold water
1½ teaspoons cornstarch
1 tablespoon dry sherry
⅛ teaspoon paprika

● Thaw fish, if frozen. In a medium skillet combine milk, ½ cup water, onion, carrot, celery leaves, dillweed, salt, and pepper. Bring to boiling; reduce heat. Cover and simmer for 10 minutes.

● Carefully add fish. Return just to boiling; reduce heat. Cover and simmer gently for 6 to 10 minutes or till done. Remove fish from skillet. Cover fish to keep it warm while preparing sauce.

● For sauce, line a colander with cheesecloth. Pour cooking liquid through colander. Discard solids. Place ½ *cup* of the strained liquid in a saucepan (add water if necessary). Combine 1 tablespoon water and cornstarch. Then add it to the strained liquid. Cook and stir till thickened and bubbly. Cook and stir for 2 minutes more. Remove from heat. Stir in sherry and paprika.

● To serve, pull the fins from each fish. Arrange fish on dinner plates. Spoon some sauce onto the plates, next to fish. Pass the remaining sauce. Makes 2 servings.

Wine-Poached Fish with Vegetable Sauce

This rich-tasting sauce is made by boiling down the poaching liquid to decrease the amount and to concentrate the flavors. (Pictured on the cover.)

Cooking oil
¾ **cup dry white wine**
½ **cup water**
1 **cup sliced fresh mushrooms**
½ **cup thinly sliced carrots**
¼ **cup thinly sliced celery**
1½ **teaspoons instant chicken bouillon granules**
½ **teaspoon dried rosemary, crushed**
4 **fresh *or* frozen halibut steaks *or* other fish steaks (1 to 1½ pounds total)**

● For poaching liquid, in a lightly oiled 10-inch skillet combine dry white wine and water. Stir in mushrooms, carrots, celery, bouillon granules, and rosemary. Bring to boiling; reduce heat. Simmer, covered, for 5 minutes.

● Add fresh or frozen fish to skillet. Spoon poaching liquid over fish. Simmer, covered, till fish flakes easily when tested with a fork (see photograph, opposite). (Allow 6 to 8 minutes for fresh fish; 8 to 10 minutes for frozen fish.) Using a slotted spoon, transfer the fish and vegetables to a platter; keep warm.

● Boil the poaching liquid, uncovered, about 5 minutes or till reduced to about ⅓ cup. Spoon atop fish and vegetables. Makes 4 servings.

Poaching fish

For poaching the halibut steaks, bring the poaching liquid to a boil, then reduce the heat and simmer, covered, for 5 minutes. This allows the flavors in the poaching liquid to develop.

Gently lower the fish steaks into the poaching liquid, using a spoon or a pancake turner. Spoon the poaching liquid over the fish to moisten the surface, as shown.

Simmer, covered, till the fish tests done when tested with a fork. Use a slotted spoon or pancake turner to remove the cooked fish and vegetables from the skillet so you can reduce the poaching liquid to make the sauce.

Vegetable-Topped Halibut

6 fresh *or* frozen halibut
   steaks, cut 1 to 1¼ inches
   thick (about 3 pounds)
1 small yellow summer
   squash
1 small zucchini
1 cup sliced fresh mushrooms
½ of a small onion, sliced and
   separated into rings
1 clove garlic, minced
¼ teaspoon finely shredded
   lemon peel
1 14½-ounce can tomatoes
1 tablespoon cornstarch
¼ teaspoon dried basil,
   crushed
   Dash bottled hot
   pepper sauce

● Thaw fish, if frozen. For sauce, cut yellow squash and zucchini lengthwise in half. Then cut into ¼-inch-thick slices. (You should have 2 cups total.) In a medium saucepan combine yellow squash, zucchini, mushrooms, onion, garlic, lemon peel, ¼ cup *water,* and ⅛ teaspoon *salt.* Bring to boiling, then reduce heat. Cover and simmer about 4 minutes or till nearly tender. Drain and return vegetables to the saucepan.

● Meanwhile, place 2 cups *water* in a large skillet. Bring to boiling. Carefully add fish. Return to boiling; reduce heat. Cover and simmer gently for 8 to 15 minutes or till fish is done. Transfer fish to a platter and keep warm while finishing sauce.

● To finish sauce, cut up tomatoes. Stir together *undrained* tomatoes, cornstarch, dried basil, and pepper sauce. Then add to vegetable mixture. Cook and stir gently over medium heat till thickened and bubbly. Cook and stir gently for 2 minutes more. To serve, spoon sauce over poached fish. Makes 6 servings.

Chilled Wine-Poached Steaks

Need a cool meal on a hot summer day? Cook these steaks up to two days ahead, then top with either the Sorrel Sauce or the Avocado Sauce.

4 fresh *or* frozen cod,
   halibut, salmon, *or* shark
   steaks, cut 1 to 1¼ inches
   thick (about 2 pounds)
1½ cups water
½ cup dry white wine
1 small green onion, sliced
1 bay leaf
   Sorrel Sauce *or* Avocado
   Sauce

● Thaw fish, if frozen. In a large skillet combine water, wine, onion, and bay leaf. Bring just to boiling. Carefully add fish. Return just to boiling; reduce heat. Cover and simmer gently for 8 to 15 minutes or till fish is done. Remove fish from water. Pat the fish dry with paper towels. Cover and chill for up to 2 days.

● To serve, prepare sauce and spoon over fish. Serves 4.

Sorrel Sauce: In a small mixing bowl stir together ¼ cup plain *yogurt,* ¼ cup *mayonnaise or salad dressing,* ¼ cup finely chopped *sorrel or spinach,* 1 sliced *green onion,* ½ teaspoon prepared *horseradish,* and dash *white pepper.* If desired, cover and chill for up to 4 hours. Makes ⅔ cup.

Avocado Sauce: In a blender container or food processor bowl place 1 *avocado,* halved, seeded, peeled, and cut into chunks; ¼ cup *chicken broth;* 2 tablespoons *milk;* 1 tablespoon *lime juice;* 2 teaspoons grated *onion;* and dash *pepper.* Cover and blend or process just till smooth. Serve immediately. Makes ¾ cup.

Japanese-Style Steamed Fish

The ginger-soy sauce adds kick to this lemony fish.

2 8- to 12-ounce fresh *or* frozen scaled drawn flounder *or* rainbow trout
4 lemon slices
2 tablespoons snipped chives
1½ cups small whole fresh mushrooms
2 tablespoons soy sauce
1 tablespoon lemon juice
1 tablespoon water
1 teaspoon grated gingerroot

● Thaw fish, if frozen. In a large skillet place a large open steamer basket over 1 inch *water*. Bring water to boiling, then reduce heat to a simmer. Carefully place fish on the steamer basket. Top with lemon slices and chives, then add mushrooms.

● Cover skillet. Steam for 8 to 15 minutes or till fish is done.

● Meanwhile, for the dipping sauce, combine soy sauce, lemon juice, water, and gingerroot. Serve the sauce on the side with the steamed fish and mushrooms. Makes 2 servings.

Trout with Tarragon-Cream Sauce

If your wire rack doesn't have handles, put two or three strips of heavy or triple-thickness foil underneath the fish.

1 2- to 2½-pound fresh *or* frozen dressed lake trout, sea trout, *or* pike
   Water
2 lemon slices
   Salt
   Tarragon-Cream Sauce

● Thaw fish, if frozen. In a fish poacher or large roasting pan that has a wire rack with handles, pour in enough water to almost reach the rack. Add lemon slices. With the fish and rack *not* in the pan, bring water to boiling. Reduce heat to a simmer.

● Sprinkle the fish with salt and place it on the greased rack. Carefully lower the rack into the pan. Cover pan. Steam for 20 to 25 minutes or till fish is done.

● Meanwhile, prepare Tarragon-Cream Sauce. Lift rack with fish from pan. Use 2 wide spatulas to carefully transfer the fish to a serving platter. Pass sauce with fish. Makes 5 or 6 servings.

Tarragon-Cream Sauce: In a small saucepan combine ⅓ cup *dry white wine* and 3 tablespoons finely chopped *shallots or* thinly sliced *green onion*. Bring to boiling, then reduce heat. Simmer, uncovered, for 8 to 10 minutes or till liquid is reduced to about *3 tablespoons,* stirring occasionally.
● Combine 1 cup *light cream* and 4 teaspoons *all-purpose flour.* Then stir it into wine mixture along with ⅛ teaspoon *salt;* ⅛ teaspoon dried *tarragon,* crushed; ⅛ teaspoon *pepper.* Cook and stir over medium heat till thickened and bubbly. Cook and stir for 1 minute more. Makes 1¼ cups.

Pike and Shrimp Quenelles

The small oval quenelles (pronounced kuh-NELLS) look a little like dumplings, but they're more delicate. Serve them as a first course or as a light main dish.

4 ounces fresh *or* frozen
    shelled shrimp
4 ounces fresh *or* frozen
    skinless pike *or*
    flounder fillets
1 cup cold whipping cream
2 egg whites
¼ teaspoon dried dillweed
⅛ teaspoon salt
    Dash pepper
2 cups hot water
½ teaspoon salt
    Mushroom Sauce
    Paprika
    Parsley sprigs

● Thaw shrimp and fish, if frozen. Devein shrimp. Pat dry with paper towels. Coarsely chop shrimp and fish. In a blender container or food processor bowl place *half* of the shrimp, *half* of the fish, and *1 tablespoon* of the cream. Cover and blend or process till smooth, stopping to scrape sides as needed. Remove the mixture and set aside. Repeat with remaining shrimp and fish and *1 tablespoon* cream. Return all to container or bowl.

● Add egg whites, dillweed, ⅛ teaspoon salt, and pepper. Cover and blend or process for 5 seconds or till mixture thickens into a paste. Through the opening in the lid or with lid ajar, and with blender on slow speed, *gradually* add remaining cream. Blend or process for 30 to 60 seconds more or till thick, stopping to scrape sides as needed. Cover and chill for 2 hours.

● Grease a 12-inch skillet. To shape quenelles, dip 2 metal soup spoons into a small bowl of *hot water.* Using 1 of the hot wet spoons, scoop out about *2 tablespoons* of the fish mixture. Use the second hot wet spoon to form the mixture into a smooth, oval mound. Carefully transfer quenelle to the skillet. Repeat with remaining mixture, making a total of 16. Dip spoons in hot water before the shaping of each quenelle.

● Mix hot water and ½ teaspoon salt. Gently pour mixture down side of skillet. Bring just to boiling; reduce heat. Cover and simmer gently about 10 minutes or till set and light textured.

● Meanwhile, prepare Mushroom Sauce. Cover sauce to keep it warm. Using a slotted spoon, remove the quenelles from skillet. Drain on paper towels.

● To serve, transfer quenelles to individual plates. Spoon sauce over quenelles and sprinkle with paprika. Garnish with parsley sprigs. Makes 4 main-dish or 8 appetizer servings.

Mushroom Sauce: In a saucepan melt 1 tablespoon *butter or margarine.* Add ¼ cup finely chopped fresh *mushrooms.* Cook for 3 to 4 minutes or till tender. Stir in 1 tablespoon *all-purpose flour* and ⅛ teaspoon *salt.* Add ¾ cup *milk.* Cook and stir over medium heat till thickened and bubbly. Stir in 1 tablespoon *dry sherry.* Cook and stir for 1 minute more. Makes ¾ cup.

Fish Stroganoff

1 pound fresh *or* frozen swordfish *or* tuna steaks, *or* skinless cusk fillets (about 1 inch thick)
1½ cups sliced fresh mushrooms
½ cup chopped onion
1 clove garlic, minced
¼ cup butter *or* margarine
3 tablespoons all-purpose flour
1 tablespoon tomato paste
1 teaspoon instant chicken bouillon granules
½ teaspoon dried basil, crushed
2 tablespoons dry white wine
1 8-ounce carton dairy sour cream
Hot cooked noodles

● Thaw fish, if frozen. For steaks, remove skin and bones. Cut fish into 1-inch pieces. In a large skillet cook mushrooms, onion, and garlic in *half* of the butter about 4 minutes or till onion is tender. Using a slotted spoon, remove vegetables from skillet. Add fish to skillet. Fry over medium-high heat for 4 to 6 minutes or till done, gently lifting and turning fish occasionally but being careful not to break up pieces. Remove fish from skillet.

● For sauce, melt remaining butter or margarine in the skillet. Stir in *1 tablespoon* of the flour, tomato paste, chicken bouillon granules, basil, and ¼ teaspoon *salt.* Then stir in 1¼ cups *water.* Cook and stir mixture over medium heat till thickened and bubbly. Cook and stir for 1 minute more.

● Stir remaining flour and the wine into sour cream. Then stir it into the mixture in skillet. Cook and stir till thickened and bubbly. Return mushroom mixture and fish to skillet. Toss lightly to coat. Cook and gently turn mixture till heated through. Serve over cooked noodles. Makes 4 servings.

Fish 'n' Chips

Light, crispy, and crunchy. Use the beer batter on mild-flavored fillets such as cod or orange roughy. Or try it on smelt and have a smelt-fry party.

1 pound fresh *or* frozen skinless perch, cod, haddock, *or* halibut fillets (about ½ inch thick)
1 pound medium potatoes (about 3)
Shortening *or* cooking oil for deep-fat frying
1 cup all-purpose flour
1 cup beer
1 egg
½ teaspoon baking powder
¼ teaspoon salt
Tartar Sauce (see recipe, page 46) (optional)
Malt vinegar *or* cider vinegar (optional)
Coarse salt (optional)

● Thaw fish, if frozen; cut into 3x2-inch pieces. If necessary, pat fish dry with paper towels. Cover and refrigerate till needed.

● For chips, cut the potatoes lengthwise into about ⅜-inch-wide strips. Pat dry with paper towels. In a 3-quart saucepan or deep-fat fryer heat 2 inches of shortening or cooking oil to 375°. Fry potatoes, ¼ at a time, for 4 to 6 minutes or till *lightly* browned. Remove potatoes and drain on paper towels. Transfer potatoes to a wire rack on a baking sheet. Spread potatoes into a single layer. Keep warm in a 300° oven while frying fish.

● Meanwhile, for batter, in a medium mixing bowl combine flour, beer, egg, baking powder, and salt. Beat with a rotary beater or wire whisk till smooth. Dip fish into batter. Then fry in the hot fat (375°) till done and coating is golden brown, turning once (allow 3 to 4 minutes total for fillets, 1 to 1½ minutes total for smelt). Remove fish and drain on paper towels. Transfer fish to another baking sheet. Keep it warm in the oven till all of fish is fried. If desired, serve Tartar Sauce for dipping or vinegar and coarse salt to sprinkle on top of fish and chips. Serves 4.

Tartar Sauce
(see recipe, page 46)

Fish 'n' Chips

Fish Marsala

Just add steamed carrots and broccoli and you've got an attractive meal.

1 pound fresh *or* frozen skinless cod, grouper, pollack, *or* whiting fillets (¾ to 1 inch thick)
Nonstick spray coating
1½ cups sliced fresh mushrooms
3 green onions, sliced
¾ cup chicken broth
¼ cup dry marsala *or* dry sherry

● Thaw fish, if frozen; cut lengthwise into 2½-inch-wide strips. Spray a *cold* medium skillet with nonstick coating. Add fish to the skillet in a single layer. Cook over medium heat till fish is done, turning once (allow 8 to 10 minutes total). Remove fish from skillet. Cover fish to keep warm while preparing sauce.

● For sauce, in the skillet cook mushrooms and green onions in *2 tablespoons* of the chicken broth for 3 to 4 minutes or till tender. Remove vegetables from skillet; set aside.

● Add marsala or sherry and remaining broth to the skillet. Bring mixture to boiling, then reduce heat. Boil gently, uncovered, about 6 minutes or till liquid is reduced to ⅓ *cup*. Stir in vegetables, then arrange fish on top. Cover and cook about 1 minute or till heated through. Makes 4 servings.

Salmon with Almonds and Pecans

Also try the creamy buttery Beurre Blanc Sauce on vegetables or eggs.

1 pound fresh *or* frozen skinless salmon fillets (¾ to 1 inch thick)
Beurre Blanc Sauce
2 tablespoons all-purpose flour
1 tablespoon cooking oil
¼ cup water
⅓ cup sliced almonds, toasted, *or* coarsely chopped macadamia nuts, toasted
⅓ cup pecan halves

● Thaw fish, if frozen; cut into 4 equal portions. Prepare Beurre Blanc Sauce; set aside. Dip fish pieces into flour, turning to coat.

● In a medium skillet heat oil. (If necessary, add more oil during frying.) Add fish to the skillet. Fry over medium heat till fish is done, turning once (allow 8 to 10 minutes total). Remove skillet from heat. Remove salmon from skillet; cover to keep warm.

● Add water to the skillet. Stir for 1 to 2 minutes, scraping up any brown bits from bottom of skillet. Add Beurre Blanc Sauce and return skillet to heat. Heat mixture through, but *do not boil*. Stir in nuts. Spoon mixture over salmon. Serves 4.

Beurre Blanc Sauce: In a small saucepan combine ¼ cup dry *white wine*, 2 tablespoons *white vinegar*, 2 tablespoons *water*, 2 tablespoons chopped *shallots or* sliced *green onion*, and dash *white pepper*. Bring to boiling, then reduce heat. Simmer, uncovered, for 8 to 10 minutes or till reduced to *half* (about ¼ cup). Remove from heat. Using a wire whisk, stir in ½ cup *butter or margarine*, 1 tablespoon at a time, till butter is melted. If desired, stir in 1 tablespoon snipped *chives*. Makes ¾ cup.

Fish Foo Yong

Fish Foo Yong, Fish Foo Yong, Fish Foo Yong—now say that FAST three times! Whether you can or can't, you'll want to savor every bite slowly.

6 ounces fresh *or* frozen
   skinless perch, cod,
   haddock, *or* halibut fillets
½ cup finely chopped Chinese
   cabbage *or* cabbage
¼ cup chopped onion
¼ cup chopped green pepper
3 tablespoons cooking oil
1 tablespoon cornstarch
1 teaspoon instant chicken
   bouillon granules
½ teaspoon grated gingerroot
   or ¼ teaspoon ground
   ginger
1 cup cold water
1 tablespoon soy sauce
1 teaspoon molasses
3 beaten eggs
¼ teaspoon salt
⅛ teaspoon pepper
1 cup coarsely chopped fresh
   or canned bean sprouts

● Thaw fish, if frozen. In a large skillet cook cabbage, onion, and green pepper in *1 tablespoon* of the cooking oil about 2 minutes or till nearly tender. Remove from heat; cool slightly.

● Meanwhile, for the sauce, in a small saucepan combine the cornstarch, bouillon granules, and gingerroot. Stir in water, soy sauce, and molasses. Cook and stir mixture over medium heat till thickened and bubbly. Cook and stir for 2 minutes more. Remove from heat. Cover to keep warm while frying patties.

● For egg mixture, finely chop raw fish. (You should have about ¾ cup.) In a medium mixing bowl beat together eggs, salt, and pepper. Stir in raw fish, cabbage mixture, and bean sprouts.

● In the large skillet heat *1 tablespoon* of the cooking oil. (If necessary, add more oil during frying.) For each patty, stir the egg mixture, then use about ¼ *cup* of it. Make 3 or 4 patties in the skillet, spreading the vegetables and fish so that they cover the egg as it spreads. Fry over medium heat till golden, turning once (allow about 3 minutes total). Remove from skillet and cover to keep warm. Repeat with remaining oil and egg mixture. To serve, spoon warm sauce over patties. Makes 4 servings.

Seafood Foo Yong: Prepare the Fish Foo Yong as directed above, *except* use 3 ounces finely chopped *fish* and 3 ounces finely chopped *shrimp* instead of the 6 ounces fish. (You should have about ¾ cup total of fish and shrimp.)

Monkfish with Grapes and Cashews

Simple but elegant.

1 pound skinless fresh *or*
   frozen monkfish *or* sea
   bass fillets (1 inch thick)
3 tablespoons butter *or*
   margarine
¾ cup seedless grapes, halved
½ cup cashews
½ teaspoon finely shredded
   orange peel
3 tablespoons orange juice

● Thaw fish, if frozen; cut into 1-inch pieces. In a large skillet heat butter or margarine. Add fish to the skillet. Fry over medium-high heat for 4 to 6 minutes or till done, gently lifting and turning the fish occasionally but being careful not to break up pieces. Gently transfer to a heated platter. Cover to keep warm.

● In the same skillet add grapes, cashews, orange peel, and orange juice. Cook and stir till heated through. Spoon over fish. Makes 4 servings.

Lime Scallops Amandine

The size of the food you stir-fry affects its cooking time. For this dish, if you use sea scallops, instead of the smaller bay scallops, halve or quarter them before stir-frying.

1 pound fresh *or* frozen
   scallops
1 cup cold water
½ teaspoon finely shredded
   lime peel
3 tablespoons lime juice
2 tablespoons cornstarch
1 teaspoon sugar
1 teaspoon salt
1 teaspoon instant chicken
   bouillon granules
1 medium cucumber, very
   thinly sliced
1 tablespoon cooking oil
½ pound fresh broccoli,
   cut up (2 cups)
1 medium sweet red *or*
   green pepper, cut into
   ¾-inch pieces (¾ cup)
¼ cup sliced almonds

● Thaw scallops, if frozen. Cut any large scallops into bite-size pieces. For sauce, stir together water, lime peel, lime juice, cornstarch, sugar, salt, chicken bouillon granules, and ⅛ teaspoon *pepper*. Set aside. Arrange cucumber slices on a serving platter. Set aside.

● Preheat a wok or large skillet over high heat; add cooking oil. (Add more oil as necessary during cooking.) Stir-fry broccoli in hot oil for 1½ minutes. Add sweet red or green pepper; stir-fry about 1½ minutes or till vegetables are crisp-tender. Remove vegetables from the wok.

● Add *half* of the scallops to the hot wok or skillet. Stir-fry scallops for 2 to 3 minutes or till opaque. Remove scallops. Stir-fry remaining scallops for 2 to 3 minutes or till opaque. Remove scallops from the wok.

● Stir sauce; add to the wok or skillet. Cook and stir till thickened and bubbly. Cook and stir for 2 minutes more. Return scallops and vegetables to the wok; stir ingredients together to coat with sauce. Cook and stir for 1 minute. Stir in almonds. Serve immediately atop cucumber slices. Makes 4 servings.

Shrimp and Apple Stir-Fry

When a recipe calls for chicken broth, you may use homemade broth, canned broth, or bouillon. Canned broth and bouillon will add more salt to the dish, however.

1 pound fresh *or* frozen
   shrimp in shells
¼ cup dry sherry
¼ cup chicken broth
2 teaspoons cornstarch
1 tablespoon cooking oil
5 green onions, bias-sliced
   into 1-inch lengths (1 cup)
2 small red apples, sliced into
   thin wedges (1½ cups)
6 ounces seedless green
   grapes, halved (1 cup)

● Thaw shrimp, if frozen. Shell and devein shrimp. Halve shrimp lengthwise. (If shrimp are large, halve them again crosswise.) For sauce, stir together the dry sherry, chicken both, and cornstarch. Set mixture aside.

● Preheat a wok or large skillet over high heat; add cooking oil. (Add more oil as necessary during cooking.) Stir-fry green onions in hot oil about 1½ minutes or till crisp-tender. Remove green onions from the wok or skillet.

● Add *half* of the shrimp to the hot wok or skillet. Stir-fry shrimp for 2 to 3 minutes or till shrimp turn pink. Remove shrimp. Stir-fry remaining shrimp for 2 to 3 minutes. Return all shrimp to the wok. Push shrimp from center of the wok.

● Stir sauce; add to center of the wok or skillet. Cook and stir till thickened and bubbly. Cook and stir for 1 minute more. Return green onions; stir ingredients together to coat with sauce. Stir in apple slices and halved grapes. Cover and cook for 1 minute. Serve immediately. Makes 4 servings.

Lime Scallops Amandine

Crab and Pork Stir-Fry

Prevent the crab from shredding into small pieces by gently stirring it into the pork mixture.

½ pound pork tenderloin
1 6-ounce package frozen
   crab meat, thawed
1 cup chicken broth
2 tablespoons soy sauce
1 tablespoon cornstarch
1 tablespoon dry sherry
1 tablespoon cooking oil
2 cloves garlic, minced
2 medium carrots, thinly
   bias sliced (1 cup)
2 cups fresh pea pods *or*
   one 6-ounce package
   frozen pea pods, thawed
   Hot cooked rice

● Partially freeze pork; cut on the bias into thin slices. Cut crab into bite-size pieces. For sauce, stir together chicken broth, soy sauce, cornstarch, and sherry. Set aside.

● Preheat a wok or large skillet over high heat; add cooking oil. (Add more oil as necessary during cooking.) Stir-fry garlic in hot oil for 15 seconds. Add carrots; stir-fry for 2 minutes. Add pea pods; stir-fry about 2 minutes or till vegetables are crisp-tender. Remove vegetables from the wok.

● Add all the pork to the hot wok or skillet. Stir-fry pork about 3 minutes or till no longer pink. Push pork from center of the wok or skillet.

● Stir sauce; add to center of the wok or skillet. Cook and stir till thickened and bubbly. Cook and stir for 2 minutes more. Return vegetables to the wok or skillet; stir ingredients together to coat with sauce. Gently stir in crab. Cover and cook for 1 minute. Serve immediately over rice. Makes 4 servings.

Scallops and Grapes

The sweetness of the currant jelly complements the tartness of lemon juice in this fruity stir-fry.

1 pound fresh *or* frozen
   scallops
⅓ cup cold water
3 tablespoons currant jelly
2 tablespoons lemon juice
2 teaspoons cornstarch
1 teaspoon instant chicken
   bouillon granules
1 tablespoon cooking oil
6 ounces fresh mushrooms,
   sliced (2 cups)
½ pound seedless red *or*
   green grapes, halved
   (1⅓ cups)
   Hot cooked rice

● Thaw scallops, if frozen. Cut any large scallops into bite-size pieces. For sauce, stir together water, currant jelly, lemon juice, cornstarch, and bouillon granules. Set aside.

● Preheat a wok or large skillet over high heat; add cooking oil. (Add more oil as necessary during cooking.) Stir-fry mushrooms about 1 minute or till done. Remove mushrooms from the wok or skillet.

● Add *half* of the scallops to the hot wok or skillet. Stir-fry scallops for 2 to 3 minutes or till opaque. Remove scallops. Stir-fry remaining scallops for 2 to 3 minutes or till opaque. Remove scallops from the wok or skillet.

● Stir sauce; add to the wok. Cook and stir till thickened and bubbly. Cook and stir for 1 minute more. Return scallops and mushrooms to the wok or skillet; stir ingredients together to coat with sauce. Stir in grapes. Cover and cook for 1 minute. Serve immediately over hot cooked rice. Makes 4 servings.

Shrimp Creole Stir-Fry

Creole cooking combines the best of French cuisine with spicy Spanish seasonings and incorporates foods readily available in Louisiana and the Gulf States.

1½ pounds fresh *or* frozen shrimp in shells
1 16-ounce can stewed tomatoes
2 tablespoons snipped parsley
2 tablespoons tomato paste
1 tablespoon cornstarch
½ teaspoon bottled hot pepper sauce
1 tablespoon cooking oil
2 cloves garlic, minced
⅛ teaspoon dried thyme, crushed
Dash ground cloves
2 stalks celery, thinly bias sliced (1 cup)
1 medium onion, chopped
1 medium green pepper, chopped (¾ cup)
1 10-ounce package frozen cut okra, thawed
Hot cooked rice

● Thaw shrimp, if frozen. Shell and devein shrimp. Halve shrimp lengthwise. (If shrimp are large, halve them again crosswise.) For sauce, stir together the *undrained* stewed tomatoes, parsley, tomato paste, cornstarch, hot pepper sauce, and ⅓ cup *cold water*. Set mixture aside.

● Preheat a wok or large skillet over high heat; add cooking oil. (Add more oil as necessary during cooking.) Stir-fry garlic, thyme, and cloves in hot oil for 15 seconds. Add celery and onion; stir-fry for 1½ minutes. Add green pepper; stir-fry about 1½ minutes or till vegetables are crisp-tender. Remove vegetables from the wok.

● Add okra to the hot wok or skillet; stir-fry about 3 minutes or till crisp-tender. Remove okra from the wok.

● Add *half* of the shrimp to the hot wok or skillet. Stir-fry for 2 to 3 minutes or till shrimp turns pink. Remove shrimp. Stir-fry the remaining shrimp for 2 to 3 minutes. Remove shrimp.

● Stir sauce; add to the wok. Cook and stir till thickened and bubbly. Cook and stir for 2 minutes more. Return vegetables and okra; stir ingredients together to coat with sauce. Reduce heat. Cover and cook for 3 minutes. Stir in shrimp. Cover and cook for 1 minute. Serve immediately over rice. If desired, pass additional hot pepper sauce. Makes 6 servings.

Shrimp with Hoisin Sauce

You may use one 10-ounce package of frozen cut asparagus instead of fresh asparagus. If you do, thaw the asparagus first, then stir-fry it for only 1½ minutes before adding the green onions.

1 pound fresh *or* frozen shrimp in shells
3 tablespoons cold water
2 tablespoons dry sherry
2 tablespoons hoisin sauce
1 teaspoon cornstarch
1 tablespoon cooking oil
1 pound asparagus, bias-sliced into 1-inch lengths (2 cups)
5 green onions, bias-sliced into 1-inch lengths (1 cup)
1 8-ounce can bamboo shoots, drained

● Thaw shrimp, if frozen. Shell and devein shrimp. Halve shrimp lengthwise. (If shrimp are large, halve them again crosswise.) For sauce, stir together the cold water, dry sherry, hoisin sauce, and cornstarch. Set mixture aside.

● Preheat a wok or large skillet over high heat; add cooking oil. (Add more oil as necessary during cooking.) Stir-fry asparagus in hot oil for 5 minutes. Add green onions; stir-fry about 1½ minutes or till vegetables are crisp-tender. Remove vegetables.

● Add *half* of the shrimp to the hot wok. Stir-fry for 2 to 3 minutes or till shrimp turns pink. Remove shrimp. Stir-fry remaining shrimp for 2 to 3 minutes. Return all shrimp to the wok. Stir in bamboo shoots. Push shrimp mixture from center.

● Stir sauce; add to center of the wok. Cook and stir till thickened and bubbly. Cook and stir for 1 minute more. Return vegetables; stir ingredients together to coat with sauce. Cook and stir for 1 minute. Serve immediately. Makes 4 servings.

Bouillabaisse

Bouillabaisse

1 dozen fresh *or* frozen clams
    or mussels in shells
2 8-ounce fresh *or* frozen
    lobster tails
12 ounces fresh *or* frozen
    skinless monkfish *or*
    red snapper fillets
1 16-ounce can tomatoes
1½ cups chicken broth
1 8-ounce bottle clam juice
2 medium leeks, sliced
½ cup dry white wine
2 tablespoons snipped parsley
2 cloves garlic, minced
1 bay leaf
½ teaspoon dried thyme,
    crushed
¼ teaspoon fennel seed,
    crushed
¼ teaspoon thread saffron,
    crushed (optional)

● Thaw clams or mussels, lobster, and fish, if frozen. Wash clams or mussels well. If necessary, debeard mussels. Combine 8 cups *water* and 3 tablespoons *salt.* Add clams or mussels; let soak for 15 minutes, then drain and rinse. Discard the water. Repeat soaking, draining, and rinsing twice.

● Meanwhile, use kitchen shears to split the lobster tails lengthwise in half, cutting through the flesh and shells. Cut the fish into 1½-inch pieces. Cover and refrigerate the shellfish and fish till needed.

● For stew, cut up tomatoes. In a 5-quart Dutch oven combine the *undrained* tomatoes, chicken broth, clam juice, leeks, wine, parsley, garlic, bay leaf, thyme, fennel, and saffron, if desired. Bring mixture to boiling, then reduce heat. Cover and simmer for 10 minutes more.

● Carefully add clams or mussels, lobster, and fish. Return just to boiling, then reduce heat. Cover and simmer gently for 3 to 6 minutes or till fish is done and clams or mussels open. Discard any unopened clams or mussels. Remove the bay leaf before serving. Makes 4 servings.

Captain's Chowder

If you like, top this tomato-pasta chowder with shredded cheddar cheese.

12 ounces fresh *or* frozen
    skinless cod, croaker,
    or red snapper fillets
1 12-ounce can (1½ cups)
    vegetable juice cocktail
½ cup medium shell macaroni
2 tablespoons grated
    Parmesan cheese
1 tablespoon dried minced
    onion
1 tablespoon instant chicken
    bouillon granules
½ teaspoon dried oregano,
    crushed
¼ teaspoon dried basil,
    crushed
    Dash garlic powder
1 cup frozen mixed vegetables

● Thaw fish, if frozen. In a large saucepan mix 3 cups *water,* vegetable juice cocktail, macaroni, Parmesan cheese, onion, bouillon granules, oregano, basil, and garlic powder. Bring to boiling; reduce heat. Cover and simmer for 15 minutes. Add vegetables. Return to boiling; reduce heat. Cover and simmer 15 minutes more or till macaroni and vegetables are tender.

● Meanwhile, measure thickness of fish. Cut fish into 1-inch pieces. Carefully add the fish to the soup mixture. Return just to boiling, then reduce heat. Cover and simmer gently till fish is done (allow about 2 minutes per ½-inch thickness of fish). To serve, ladle soup into individual soup bowls. Makes 4 servings.

Seafood Chili Soup

Tastes just like Texas chili, but without the beef.

1 pound fresh *or* frozen
 skinless cod, cusk, *or*
 monkfish fillets
¼ cup chopped onion
¼ cup chopped green pepper
1 clove garlic, minced
1 tablespoon cooking oil
1 12-ounce can (1½ cups)
 tomato juice
1 8-ounce can red kidney
 beans
1 7½-ounce can tomatoes,
 cut up
1 6-ounce can sliced mushrooms, drained
1 tablespoon chili powder
½ teaspoon sugar
¼ teaspoon dried basil,
 crushed
⅛ to ¼ teaspoon crushed red
 pepper
1 bay leaf

● Thaw fish, if frozen. In a medium saucepan cook onion, green pepper, and garlic in cooking oil till vegetables are tender.

● Stir in the tomato juice, *undrained* kidney beans, *undrained* tomatoes, mushrooms, chili powder, sugar, basil, red pepper, bay leaf, 1 cup *water,* and ½ teaspoon *salt.* Bring to boiling; reduce heat. Cover and simmer for 15 minutes.

● Meanwhile, measure thickness of fish. Cut fish into 1-inch pieces. Carefully add fish to soup mixture. Return mixture just to boiling, then reduce heat. Cover and simmer gently till fish is done (allow about 2 minutes per ½-inch thickness of fish).

● To serve, remove bay leaf. Ladle soup into individual soup bowls. If desired, top with dairy sour cream. Makes 4 servings.

Salmon and Tomato Bisque

12 ounces fresh *or* frozen
 salmon, halibut, *or*
 swordfish steaks, cut
 1 inch thick
1½ cups sliced fresh
 mushrooms
½ cup chopped onion
2 tablespoons butter *or*
 margarine
1 14½-ounce can tomatoes,
 finely cut up
¾ cup chicken broth
¼ teaspoon salt
¼ teaspoon dried dillweed
 Dash pepper
1½ cups light cream *or* milk
2 tablespoons cornstarch
2 tablespoons dry sherry
 Fresh dill (optional)

● Thaw fish, if frozen. Remove skin and bones from fish. Cut fish into ¾-inch pieces.

● In a medium saucepan cook mushrooms and onion in butter till tender. Stir in tomatoes, chicken broth, salt, dillweed, and pepper. Bring mixture just to boiling. Carefully add the fish. Return the tomato mixture just to boiling, then reduce heat. Cover and simmer gently about 4 minutes or till fish is done.

● Meanwhile, in a small saucepan combine cream or milk and cornstarch. Cook and stir over medium heat till thickened and bubbly. Cook and stir for 2 minutes more. Gently stir cream mixture into tomato mixture. Then gently stir in the sherry. If necessary, cook mixture over medium-low heat till heated through. *Do not boil.*

● To serve, ladle soup into individual soup bowls. If desired, garnish with fresh dill. Makes 4 servings.

Landlubber's Chowder

Whether you're on land or at sea, this colorful, creamy chowder is sure to be a hit.

12 ounces fresh *or* frozen
salmon *or* swordfish
steaks, cut ¾ inch thick
1 medium tomato
3 slices bacon, halved
½ cup chopped onion
¼ cup chopped celery
1 cup water
1 cup loose-pack frozen
mixed broccoli, carrots,
and cauliflower
¾ cup cubed peeled potato
1 tablespoon instant chicken
bouillon granules
1 teaspoon Worcester-
shire sauce
⅛ teaspoon pepper
½ cup light cream
2 tablespoons all-purpose
flour
1¼ cups milk

● Thaw fish, if frozen; remove skin and bones. Cut fish into ¾-inch pieces. Cover and refrigerate till needed. Cut tomato into 8 wedges, then seed and cut wedges crosswise in half. Set aside.

● In a large saucepan cook the bacon till crisp. Drain, reserving *1 tablespoon* of drippings. Crumble bacon and set aside. Cook onion and celery in reserved drippings till nearly tender.

● Stir in water, frozen vegetables, potato, bouillon granules, Worcestershire sauce, and pepper. Bring to boiling, then reduce heat. Cover and simmer for 5 minutes.

● Combine cream and flour, then add it to potato mixture in pan. Stir in milk. Add fish. Bring almost to boiling, then reduce heat. Cover and simmer gently about 3 minutes or till fish is done. *Do not boil.* Stir in bacon and tomato. Makes 4 servings.

Ragout de Sole

The delicate orange flavor is a pleasant surprise.

8 ounces fresh *or* frozen
skinless sole *or* orange
roughy fillets (about ½
inch thick)
8 ounces fresh *or* frozen
shelled shrimp
1 8-ounce package frozen cut
asparagus
3 cups milk
2 tablespoons all-purpose
flour
1 cup sliced fresh mushrooms
1 green onion, thinly sliced
½ teaspoon finely shredded
orange peel
¼ teaspoon salt
⅛ teaspoon white pepper
1 cup cooked rice
2 tablespoons orange juice

● Thaw fish and shrimp, if frozen. Cut fish into 1-inch pieces. Devein shrimp. Cover and refrigerate fish and shrimp till needed. Cook asparagus according to package directions, then drain and set asparagus aside.

● In a large saucepan combine about ¼ *cup* of the milk and flour till smooth, then stir in the remaining milk. Add fish, shrimp, mushrooms, onion, orange peel, salt, and pepper. Bring almost to boiling, then reduce heat. Cover and simmer gently for 2 to 3 minutes or till fish is done and shrimp turn pink. *Do not boil.* Stir in cooked asparagus, rice, and orange juice, and heat through. Makes 5 servings.

In-a-Hurry Curried Seafood Chowder

For a meal in minutes, start with a can of soup, then add apple, fish, sour cream, and nuts.

12 ounces fresh *or* frozen
  skinless cod, monkfish,
  or tilefish fillets
 1 cup milk
 1 10¾-ounce can condensed
  New England clam
  chowder
 1 medium apple, cored and
  chopped
 1 teaspoon curry powder
 1 teaspoon lemon juice
 ½ cup dairy sour cream
  Chopped peanuts

● Thaw fish, if frozen. Measure thickness of fish; cut into 1-inch pieces. Cover and refrigerate the fish till needed.

● In a medium saucepan stir milk into clam chowder. Stir in apple, curry powder, and lemon juice. Bring almost to boiling. Carefully add fish to soup mixture. Return almost to boiling, then reduce heat. Cover and simmer gently till the fish is done (allow about 2 minutes per ½-inch thickness of fish).

● Stir in sour cream and heat through. Ladle the soup into individual soup bowls and sprinkle with peanuts. Serves 3.

Seafood Gumbo

The full flavor of catfish is a good choice for this well-seasoned gumbo, too.

12 ounces fresh *or* frozen
  cooked split crab legs
 8 ounces fresh *or* frozen
  shelled shrimp
 1 pound fresh *or* frozen
  orange roughy fillets
  (½ to 1 inch thick)
 ½ cup margarine
 ½ cup all-purpose flour
 2 cups chopped onion
 1 cup chopped green pepper
 5 cloves garlic, minced
 4 cups chicken broth
 1 28-ounce can tomatoes,
  cut up
 2 cups sliced okra *or* one 10-
  ounce package frozen cut
  okra, thawed
 1 teaspoon dried thyme,
  crushed
 ½ teaspoon ground red pepper
 1 bay leaf
 2 teaspoons filé powder
 4 cups hot cooked rice

● Thaw crab, shrimp, and fish, if frozen. Remove crabmeat from shells, then cut crabmeat into bite-size pieces. Devein shrimp. Cut fish into 1-inch pieces. Cover and refrigerate the shellfish and fish till needed.

● For gumbo, in a 5-quart heavy Dutch oven melt margarine. Stir in flour. Cook and stir over medium-low heat for 20 to 25 minutes or till a dark reddish brown roux is formed. Add onion, green pepper, and garlic. Then continue cooking and stirring over medium-low heat about 15 minutes or till the vegetables are very tender.

● Gradually stir in chicken broth. Then stir in the *undrained* tomatoes, okra, thyme, pepper, and bay leaf. Bring to boiling, then reduce heat. Cover and simmer for 30 minutes.

● Carefully add crab, shrimp, and fish. Return just to boiling, then reduce heat. Cover and simmer gently for 2 to 4 minutes or till shrimp turns pink and fish is done. Remove from heat. Stir in filé powder.

● To serve, remove bay leaf. Spoon the gumbo over the hot cooked rice in individual soup bowls. Makes 8 servings.

Start with a roux (ROO) as the base for this traditional southern gumbo.

1 Combining the margarine and flour

The roux, along with the okra and filé powder, thickens the Seafood Gumbo.

Make the roux from equal parts of margarine and flour. First melt the margarine, then stir in the flour till smooth. At the beginning of cooking, the roux will be a vanilla color.

2 Cooking the roux

Cook the roux slowly over medium-low heat for 20 to 25 minutes. Be sure to stir the roux *constantly* while it's cooking so that it doesn't scorch. If the roux burns, it won't thicken the gumbo.

To judge the doneness of the roux, compare its color to that of a tarnished copper penny. The roux will have the same rich brown color as the penny, as shown at right. It will also have a nutty aroma.

Cod-Vegetable Soup

Chock-full of celery, carrot, cabbage, and zucchini.

1 pound fresh *or* frozen
    skinless cod, croaker,
    or drum fillets
½ cup sliced celery
¼ cup chopped onion
2 tablespoons butter *or*
    margarine
3 cups chicken broth
1 small zucchini, sliced ½
    inch thick (1⅓ cups)
1 cup coarsely chopped
    cabbage
1 medium carrot, thinly sliced
    (½ cup)
¼ teaspoon dried basil,
    crushed
¼ teaspoon dried thyme,
    crushed
¼ teaspoon pepper
⅛ teaspoon dried rosemary,
    crushed
    Lemon wedges (optional)

● Thaw fish, if frozen. In a large saucepan cook the celery and onion in the butter or margarine till tender.

● Stir in chicken broth, sliced zucchini, chopped cabbage, sliced carrot, basil, thyme, pepper, and rosemary. Bring mixture to boiling, then reduce heat. Cover and simmer for 5 to 8 minutes or till vegetables are nearly tender.

● Meanwhile, measure thickness of fish. Cut fish into 1-inch pieces. Carefully add the fish to broth mixture. Return just to boiling, then reduce heat. Cover and simmer gently till fish is done (allow about 2 minutes per ½-inch thickness of fish).

● To serve, ladle soup into individual soup bowls. If desired, pass lemon wedges to squeeze over soup before eating. Serves 4.

Fish 'n' Citrus Soup

Sorrel (SAW-ruhl) adds a pleasant lemony flavor and a hint of green.

1½ pounds fresh *or* frozen
      skinless cusk, haddock,
      or pike fillets, *or*
      halibut *or* shark steaks
3   cups chicken broth
1   teaspoon finely shredded
      orange peel
⅓   cup orange juice
¼   cup chopped onion
1   tablespoon soy sauce
⅛   teaspoon white pepper
2   cloves garlic, minced
1   bay leaf
1   cup finely chopped sorrel *or*
      spinach

● Thaw fish, if frozen. In a large saucepan combine chicken broth, orange peel, orange juice, onion, soy sauce, pepper, garlic, and bay leaf. Bring mixture to boiling, then reduce heat. Cover and simmer for 5 minutes.

● Meanwhile, if using fish steaks, remove skin and bones. Measure thickness of fish. Cut fish into 1-inch pieces. Carefully add fish to soup mixture. Return just to boiling, then reduce heat. Cover and simmer gently till fish is done (allow about 2 minutes per ½-inch thickness of fish). Remove from heat. Remove bay leaf. Gently stir in sorrel or spinach till wilted. Makes 4 servings.

Cod-Vegetable Soup

Super Salad Bowls

½ cup wheat berries
¼ cup chopped celery
⅓ cup mayonnaise *or* salad dressing
⅓ cup plain yogurt
2 tablespoons thinly sliced green onion
1 teaspoon snipped fresh dill *or* ¼ teaspoon dried dillweed
½ teaspoon dried basil, crushed
⅛ teaspoon pepper
3 heads Bibb lettuce
1 7-ounce can solid white tuna, drained
2 small carrots, shredded
8 radishes, shredded
1 tablespoon milk

● In a small saucepan combine wheat berries and 2 cups *water*. Bring to boiling, then reduce heat. Cover and simmer for 1 hour. Drain and cool. In a medium mixing bowl combine the wheat berries and celery.

● For dressing, in a small mixing bowl combine mayonnaise or salad dressing, yogurt, onion, dill, basil, and pepper. Stir till well blended. Add *half* of the dressing mixture to the wheat berry mixture and toss lightly to coat. Cover and chill the wheat berry mixture and the remaining dressing separately.

● For salads, remove centers from heads of lettuce, leaving the outer leaves intact to form bowls. (Reserve centers for another use.) Place the lettuce bowls on 3 dinner plates. Break tuna into chunks. Arrange the wheat berry mixture, tuna, carrots, and radishes in separate piles in the lettuce bowls. If desired, garnish salads with additional fresh dill. If necessary, stir milk into the remaining dressing to make it of drizzling consistency. Serve remaining dressing separately. Makes 3 servings.

Aioli Platter

2 large carrots
1 9-ounce package frozen artichoke hearts
2 4- to 6-ounce fresh halibut steaks (cut 1 inch thick)
½ cup dry white wine
1 egg
2 tablespoons lemon juice
3 *or* 4 cloves garlic, chopped
¼ teaspoon salt
½ cup salad oil
½ cup olive oil
  Romaine leaves
4 hard-cooked eggs, sliced
1 cup whole fresh mushrooms
1 cup cherry tomatoes, halved
½ cup pitted ripe olives
  Milk
  Snipped chives (optional)

● Cut carrots crosswise in half, then cut pieces lengthwise in half. In a medium covered saucepan cook carrots and artichoke hearts in a small amount of lightly salted boiling water about 10 minutes or till vegetables are nearly tender, then drain. Rinse with cold water, then drain again. Cover and chill.

● Place fish in a small skillet. Add wine. Bring to boiling; reduce heat. Cover and simmer about 6 minutes or till fish flakes easily with a fork. Drain fish, cool, break into chunks, then chill.

● For dressing, in a blender container or food processor bowl combine the 1 egg, lemon juice, garlic, and salt. Cover and blend or process for 5 seconds. Through opening in lid and with blender or processor on slow speed, *gradually* add salad oil in a thin stream. (When necessary, stop blender and scrape sides.) Then on slow speed, *gradually* add olive oil in a thin stream.

● For salad, line a medium platter with romaine leaves. Arrange carrots, artichokes, fish, egg slices, mushrooms, tomatoes, and olives on the platter. If necessary, stir a few tablespoons of milk into dressing to make it of drizzling consistency. Drizzle some of the dressing over salad. If desired, sprinkle with snipped chives. Serve the remaining dressing separately. Makes 4 servings.

Super Salad Bowls

Sweet-and-Sour Pasta Salad

To keep the broccoli bright green and the nuts crunchy, add them just before serving.

- 1 tablespoon cornstarch
- 1 tablespoon brown sugar
- ½ teaspoon ground ginger
- ¼ teaspoon garlic powder
- 1 6-ounce can unsweetened pineapple juice
- ¼ cup white wine vinegar
- 2 tablespoons water
- 2 tablespoons soy sauce
- 1½ cups broccoli flowerets
- 2 cups pasta bow ties
- 1 8-ounce package frozen cooked shrimp, thawed
- 1 medium carrot, thinly bias sliced
- ½ cup peanuts *or* cashews

● For dressing, in a small saucepan combine cornstarch, sugar, ginger, and garlic powder. Stir in juice, vinegar, water, and soy sauce. Cook and stir till thickened and bubbly. Cook and stir for 2 minutes more. Remove from heat and cool.

● Meanwhile, in a medium covered saucepan cook broccoli in a small amount of lightly salted boiling water for 4 to 5 minutes or till nearly tender, then drain. Rinse with cold water, then drain again. Cover and chill.

● In another saucepan cook pasta according to package directions, then drain. Rinse with cold water, then drain again.

● In a medium salad bowl combine pasta, shrimp, and carrot. Pour dressing over pasta mixture and toss lightly to coat. Cover and chill for 2 to 8 hours, lightly tossing mixture occasionally.

● To serve, add chilled broccoli and peanuts or cashews. Toss lightly to mix. Makes 4 servings.

Crab and Kiwi-Fruit Salads

Company coming? Here's an easy but elegant idea. Just serve with a few sesame toast crackers and iced tea, and you've got a complete meal.

- ⅔ cup mayonnaise *or* salad dressing
- 2 tablespoons thinly sliced green onion
- 2 teaspoons lemon juice
- ½ teaspoon ground ginger Dash ground red pepper
- 2 8-ounce packages frozen salad-style crab-flavored fish, thawed
- 4 kiwi fruits, peeled and sliced crosswise
- ¼ cup sliced almonds, toasted

● In a medium mixing bowl combine mayonnaise or salad dressing, green onion, lemon juice, ginger, and red pepper. Stir till well blended.

● Fold crab-flavored fish into mayonnaise mixture. If desired, cover and chill for up to 6 hours.

● For salads, overlap kiwi slices around the outer edges of 4 salad plates. Spoon crab mixture onto centers of plates. Sprinkle with almonds. Makes 4 servings.

Avocado and Seafood Salad

The crab-flavored fish sticks are sometimes called surimi. This "seafood" is actually a blend of whitefish and crabmeat.

½ cup dairy sour cream
2 tablespoons frozen orange
   juice concentrate, thawed
1 to 2 tablespoons milk
2 8-ounce packages frozen
   crab-flavored fish sticks,
   thawed and cut into 1-inch
   pieces
3 cups torn Bibb lettuce *or*
   Boston lettuce
1 cup torn escarole
1 11-ounce can mandarin
   orange sections, drained
¼ cup sliced almonds, toasted
1 avocado, seeded, peeled,
   and sliced crosswise

● For dressing, in a mixing bowl combine sour cream and orange juice concentrate. Stir till well blended. Stir in enough milk to make dressing of desired consistency. Cover and chill.

● For salad, in a large salad bowl combine fish pieces, lettuce, escarole, orange sections, and almonds. Add avocado slices. Pour dressing over lettuce mixture and toss lightly to coat. Makes 4 servings.

Preparing an avocado

To remove the seed from an avocado, cut the fruit lengthwise around the seed. Then, with your hands, gently twist the halves in opposite directions to separate.

Carefully tap the seed with the cutting edge of a sharp knife so the blade is caught in the seed. Rotate the knife to loosen the seed, then use the knife to lift the seed out, as shown.

To peel the avocado, place it cut side down in your palm. Use the sharp knife to loosen and strip the skin from the fruit.

Tuna and Pasta Salad

Our Test Kitchen also suggests serving this colorful salad in a lettuce-lined bowl.

2 cups tiny shell macaroni
1 12½-ounce can tuna,
    drained and flaked
½ cup shredded Swiss cheese
½ cup shredded cheddar
    cheese
1 stalk celery, sliced
¼ cup sliced green onion
½ cup mayonnaise *or* salad
    dressing
½ cup plain yogurt
1 tablespoon milk
½ teaspoon garlic salt
½ teaspoon dried dillweed
    Milk
1 medium tomato, seeded and
    cut into thin strips
    Bibb lettuce *or* Boston
    lettuce leaves
    Lemon *or* lime wedges

● Cook shell macaroni according to package directions, then drain. Rinse with cold water, then drain again.

● In a medium mixing bowl combine pasta, tuna, Swiss cheese, cheddar cheese, celery, and green onion.

● For dressing, in a small mixing bowl combine the mayonnaise or salad dressing, yogurt, 1 tablespoon milk, garlic salt, and dillweed. Stir till well blended. Pour dressing over pasta mixture and toss lightly to coat. Cover and chill for 2 to 8 hours.

● To serve, if necessary, stir in a few tablespoons of additional milk to moisten mixture. Add tomato and toss lightly. Line 6 salad plates with lettuce. Spoon pasta mixture onto the plates. Garnish with lemon or lime wedges. Makes 6 servings.

Tossed Salade Niçoise

Pronounced sah-LAHD nee-SWAHZ, this Mediterranean salad makes either 12 appetizer or 6 to 8 main-dish servings.

2 medium potatoes, peeled
    and sliced ¼ inch thick
1 9-ounce package frozen cut
    green beans
1 cup cherry tomatoes, halved
1 small green pepper, seeded
    and cut into strips
¼ cup sliced pitted ripe olives
¾ cup clear Italian salad
    dressing
4 cups torn romaine
3 cups torn Bibb lettuce *or*
    Boston lettuce
1 9¼-ounce can water-packed
    tuna, drained, flaked, and
    chilled
2 hard-cooked eggs, sliced
1 2-ounce can anchovy fillets,
    drained

● In a medium covered saucepan cook potatoes in lightly salted boiling water for 5 minutes. Break up the frozen beans and add them to the potatoes in the saucepan. Return to boiling. Cover and boil gently for 4 to 6 minutes more or till nearly tender, then drain. Cool vegetables slightly.

● In a very large salad bowl combine potatoes, green beans, tomatoes, green pepper, and olives. Pour dressing over vegetables. Toss lightly to coat. Cover and chill for 2 to 3 hours.

● To serve, add romaine, Bibb or Boston lettuce, and tuna. Toss lightly to coat. Garnish with egg slices and anchovy fillets. Makes 6 to 8 servings.

Tuna-Orange Toss

Here's a tip for a prettier salad: Use the solid white tuna because it breaks up less when the salad is tossed.

1½ teaspoons cornstarch
1½ teaspoons sugar
¼ teaspoon dry mustard
¼ teaspoon paprika
⅛ teaspoon salt
   Dash pepper
½ cup orange juice
2 tablespoons catsup
1 tablespoon salad oil
4 cups torn iceberg lettuce
1 11-ounce can mandarin
   orange sections, drained
½ of a small cucumber, sliced
⅓ cup sliced radishes
1 9¼-ounce can water-packed
   tuna, drained, broken into
   chunks, and chilled

● For dressing, in a small saucepan combine cornstarch, sugar, dry mustard, paprika, salt, and pepper. Stir in orange juice. Cook and stir till thickened and bubbly. Cook and stir for 2 minutes more. Remove from heat. Stir in the catsup and salad oil. Cover and chill.

● For salad, in a medium salad bowl combine lettuce, orange sections, cucumber, and radishes. Stir dressing and pour over mixture. Toss to coat. Add tuna and toss lightly. Serves 4.

Cod-Spinach Salad with Lemon-Mustard Dressing

Try a vegetable peeler instead of a knife to easily cut strips of peel from the lemon.

1½ pounds fresh *or* frozen cod
   fillets
¼ cup dry white wine
¼ cup water
1 egg
1 large clove garlic, quartered
2 1x½-inch strips lemon peel
3 tablespoons lemon juice
1 tablespoon Dijon-style
   mustard
½ teaspoon dried thyme,
   crushed
¼ teaspoon sugar
1 cup olive oil *or* salad oil
1 to 3 tablespoons milk
5 cups torn spinach
5 cups torn sorrel*
1½ cups sliced fresh
   mushrooms
½ cup sliced radishes
   Snipped chives

● Thaw fish, if frozen. Cut fish into 1-inch cubes. Place fish in a large skillet. Add wine, water, and ¼ teaspoon *salt*. Bring to boiling, then reduce heat. Cover and simmer for 3 to 6 minutes or till fish flakes easily with a fork. Drain and cool the fish slightly, then chill.

● For dressing, in a blender container or food processor bowl combine egg, garlic, lemon peel, lemon juice, mustard, thyme, sugar, ¼ teaspoon *salt,* and ⅛ teaspoon *pepper.* Cover and blend or process till smooth. Through the opening in the lid or with lid ajar, and with blender or food processor on slow speed, *gradually* add oil in a thin stream. (When necessary, stop blender and scrape sides.) Cover and blend about 20 seconds more or till thickened. If necessary, stir in enough milk to make dressing of desired consistency. Cover and chill.

● To serve, in a very large mixing bowl combine fish, spinach, sorrel, mushrooms, and radishes. Toss lightly to mix. Spoon spinach mixture onto 6 salad plates. Drizzle with dressing and sprinkle with chives. Makes 6 servings.

*If sorrel is unavailable, substitute additional spinach.

By-the-Seashore Salmon Shells

Take a bite and close your eyes—you just might hear the waves hitting the rocks.

12 large shell macaroni
3 hard-cooked eggs
½ cup creamy buttermilk
  salad dressing
¼ teaspoon dried dillweed
1 15½-ounce can salmon,
  drained, skin and bones
  removed, flaked, and
  chilled
½ cup thinly sliced celery
4 cups shredded iceberg
  lettuce
1 medium green pepper,
  seeded and cut into strips
1 medium tomato, seeded and
  chopped
  Creamy buttermilk salad
  dressing

● Cook pasta shells according to package directions, then drain. Rinse with cold water, then drain again and chill.

● Meanwhile, cut hard-cooked eggs in half and remove yolks. In a medium mixing bowl mash yolks with a fork. Stir in the ½ cup buttermilk dressing and dillweed. Chop the egg whites. Add chopped egg whites, salmon, and celery to yolk mixture. Mix just till combined. If desired, cover and chill for up to 8 hours.

● In a medium mixing bowl combine shredded lettuce, green pepper, and chopped tomato. Toss lightly to mix.

● To serve, divide lettuce mixture among 4 salad plates. Spoon salmon mixture into pasta shells. Place 3 shells on top of lettuce on each plate. Serve additional buttermilk dressing separately. Makes 4 servings.

Tuna-Stuffed Tomatoes

You'll need big, plump tomatoes to hold all of this wonderful mint-tuna filling.

4 large tomatoes
¼ cup mayonnaise *or* salad
  dressing
¼ cup dairy sour cream
2 tablespoons thinly sliced
  green onion
4 teaspoons snipped fresh
  mint *or* 1½ teaspoons
  dried mint, crushed
1 12½-ounce can tuna,
  drained, broken into
  chunks, and chilled
½ cup chopped seeded
  cucumber
  Red leaf lettuce *or* alfalfa
  sprouts

● For tomato shells, cut a thin slice off the top of each tomato. Use a spoon to scoop out the seeds and pulp from each tomato, leaving a ¼-inch-thick shell. Invert shells onto paper towels to drain, then chill till serving time. Discard seeds from the scooped-out pulp. Chop the pulp, then drain. Reserve *½ cup* of the drained pulp.

● For salad mixture, in a mixing bowl combine mayonnaise or salad dressing, sour cream, onion, and mint. Stir mixture till well blended. Add tuna and toss lightly to mix. If desired, cover and chill for up to 8 hours.

● To serve, add the reserved chopped tomato and cucumber to the salad mixture. Toss lightly to mix. Line 4 salad plates with lettuce leaves or sprouts. Place tomato shells on the plates. Fill the shells with salad mixture, mounding mixture slightly. Makes 4 servings.

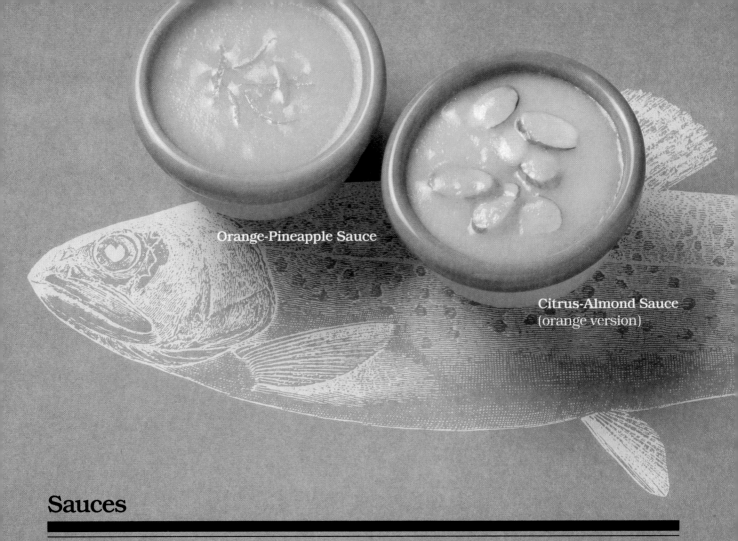

Orange-Pineapple Sauce

Citrus-Almond Sauce
(orange version)

Sauces

The eight special sauces in this section are good on any kind of fish.

Hot Citrus Sauce

Lemon or orange—what's your fancy? You pick the flavor of this sauce.

½   cup chicken broth
¼   teaspoon finely shredded
     lemon *or* orange peel
4   teaspoons lemon *or* orange
     juice
2   teaspoons cornstarch
1   tablespoon butter *or*
     margarine

● In a small saucepan combine chicken broth, peel, juice, and cornstarch. Cook and stir over medium heat till thickened and bubbly. Cook and stir for 1 minute more. Remove from heat; stir in the butter or margarine. Serve immediately. Makes ½ cup.

Citrus-Almond Sauce: Prepare Hot Citrus Sauce as directed above. Stir in 2 tablespoons sliced *almonds.* Makes ½ cup.

Lemon-Dill Sauce: Prepare Hot Citrus Sauce as directed above, using lemon peel and juice. Stir in ⅛ teaspoon dried *dillweed* before cooking. Makes ½ cup.

Orange-Pineapple Sauce: Prepare Hot Citrus Sauce as directed above, using the orange peel and juice. Stir in 1 tablespoon unsweetened *pineapple juice* before cooking. Makes ½ cup.

Tartar Sauce

Creamy Tarragon Sauce

Creamy Tarragon Sauce

Have any leftover sauce? Cover and store it in the refrigerator for up to 10 days.

1   1-ounce envelope
    hollandaise sauce mix
2   tablespoons dry white wine
½   teaspoon dried tarragon,
    crushed
½   cup mayonnaise *or* salad
    dressing

● In a small saucepan prepare sauce mix according to package directions. Remove from heat and stir in wine and tarragon. Let cool for 10 to 15 minutes.

● In a small mixing bowl fold the tarragon mixture into the mayonnaise or salad dressing. Serve sauce at room temperature. Makes 1¼ cups.

Tartar Sauce

An old standby you can mix in minutes.

1   cup mayonnaise *or* salad
    dressing
¼   cup finely chopped dill
    pickle *or* sweet pickle
    relish
1   tablespoon finely chopped
    onion
1   tablespoon snipped parsley
1   tablespoon diced pimiento
1   teaspoon lemon juice

● In a small mixing bowl combine the mayonnaise or salad dressing, dill pickle or pickle relish, onion, parsley, pimiento, and lemon juice. Stir till well blended. If desired, cover and chill to blend the flavors before serving. Makes 1 cup.

Green Chili Salsa

Cucumber-Dill Sauce

Cucumber-Dill Sauce

It's tangy but so good!

⅓ cup finely chopped, seeded, peeled cucumber
¼ cup plain yogurt
¼ cup mayonnaise *or* salad dressing
2 tablespoons milk
¼ teaspoon dried dillweed

● In a small mixing bowl combine chopped cucumber, yogurt, mayonnaise or salad dressing, milk, and dillweed. Stir till well blended. If desired, cover and chill to blend the flavors before serving. Makes ¾ cup.

Green Chili Salsa

If you like it hot, add the pepper sauce.

1 14½-ounce can sodium-free tomatoes, drained
1 4-ounce can whole green chili peppers, drained
2 tablespoons chopped onion
1 clove garlic, minced
Several dashes bottled hot pepper sauce (optional)

● In a blender container or food processor bowl place tomatoes, chili peppers, onion, garlic, and hot pepper sauce, if desired. Cover and blend or process about 5 seconds or till combined, but still chunky. Serve at room temperature, or transfer to a small saucepan and heat just till warm. Makes 1½ cups.

Index